AF522051

The Best of Bum

The Best of Bum

The Quotable Bum Phillips

Edited by David Kaplan
and Daniel Griffin

Texas Monthly Press, Inc.
P. O. Box 1569
Austin, Texas 78767

A B C D E F G H

ISBN 0-932012-13-2

Book Design by Martha Durke

"You've heard of men dying with their boots on. Well, I think Bum was born with 'em on.

—Helen (Mrs. Bum) Phillips

On being called "Bum"

"As long as it's a name and not a description, I don't mind."

On his given name, Oail

"Cain't nobody spell it or pronounce it or anything."

On the improvement of football equipment

"I had a helmet in high school you could put in your pocket."

"You can't worry in this business. There are only two kinds of coaches: those who have been fired and those who are gonna be fired."

Reading the paper Monday morning after a close defeat

"I was sort of hoping somebody had said, 'Hey, you folks were better. We're changing the score.'"

"I don't mind people thinking I'm stupid, but I don't want to give them any proof."

On whether he would ever leave Texas

"I done drew the line. Just like at the Alamo. You're either on one side of the line or the other. I don't want to ever leave Texas again. I don't see moving me and my family someplace none of us want to be. I don't want to be living around people I don't know. And don't understand."

On a poor start vs. the Giants, 1976

"We got our starting time mixed up. We started playing at 9:00 p.m. instead of 8."

Asked what he told his team at halftime to spark a great 26–23 comeback vs. New England, 1978

"I begged a little and I cried a little."

On getting through the crowd to congratulate Steeler coach, Chuck Noll, after a loss

"There was a large man with a Steeler cap on and he said, 'Come on coach, follow me.' He did a great job getting me through the people. I don't know who the man was. If I did, I'd have signed him. The way things were for us today, I'd have probably played him, too."

"You know, tryin' to run wide on us is like spittin' in the ocean."

Asked why the now-effective three–four defense was shelved when Sid Gillman was head coach

"Sid thought you could run on it. Somebody made a first down on us once."

"You have to get a football team ready to play a sixteen-game season. If you start out playing each game like it's the Super Bowl, you'll never get there. We might start a little slower than some teams, but we're gonna try to finish faster."

On whether he made an obscene gesture to unruly New Orleans fans

"The only obscene thing that happened was the way some of these fans behaved. All I did was signal them that we were number one."

On a trade that didn't materialize

"It's kinda like buying cars and selling cars. They wanted too much for their car."

On why Bum keeps the Oilers' workouts relatively short

"Most pros are married and they have to spend some time around the house. They have responsibilities to their wives. They're in the Honey-do business. You know, Honey-do this and Honey-do that. I don't want the players' wives complaining about old Bum Phillips in their pillow talk all night."

"I just do what feels natural. Some coaches feel you should drive athletes to their best performance, but you can lead me a whole lot further than you can drive me and I think most athletes are that way."

In overtime, losing the coin toss, and then the game

"It doesn't seem fair to lose because of a flip. I don't like to flip for anything and sure as hell not for a football game."

On the Oilers' new training camp in Quail Valley

"My office will be two hundred yards from my front door. Or one hundred fifty if I could cut through my neighbor's living room."

Asked if he would take a vacation after the season-ending loss to Pittsburgh, 1976

"Yeah, I'll take a little time off. I don't imagine I'll be back in the office before 8:00 a.m. Monday."

Training camp

On training camp

"I never root for a guy to lose his job. I root for somebody to win it. I like the competition. That's what this time of year is all about."

"No player has the right to hurt the other forty-four players on his team. Their individual pride or whatever it is can't come ahead of the team.

"That's why I don't get penalties on the sideline. Because there isn't any way that I can get that fifteen yards back."

After losing to St. Louis, 1979

"Before the game I thought we were in a good frame of mind. But hell, you can't stop nobody with a frame of mind."

On the Oilers' 7–0 victory over New England, 1975

"I sure like it when one player does all the scoring and he happens to be on your team."

On the draft

"We're gonna look real hard at a fella's character before we draft him. There's been a lot of people cut in this league who had the ability, more ability than guys who are playing. But they didn't have the heart."

"I don't like practice either. I'd rather coach seven games a week than one."

On complacency

"People tend to get satisfied with themselves. They think they're good, and they were—last year. This is this year."

Viewing the field in Cleveland, mostly ice with scattered patches of dirt, 1977

"Why don't we just forget it and play 'em a doubleheader next year?"

On the toughness of the Oiler defense

"Teams will know they've been up against us—bruise-wise."

"You don't give up four years of friendship over an argument. You might have a fight with a brother or sister and at that moment you don't like them at all, but deep down you love them and you recover from the fight. That's the way this football team has been."

"Pickup trucks is one of the five things in life that I know something about. That and cold beer, barbecued ribs, gumbo, and chewing tobacco."

On a Pastorini bomb

"The ball hung in the air so long, they were already back in the huddle calling the next play when it came down."

Asked if he would conduct practice outdoors to prepare for the cold and snow in New England, 1978

"No. How can you practice being miserable?"

"They assured me on the telephone that it was snowing on both sides of the fifty-yard line."

Asked if his defense intended to give up any touchdowns in 1976 after shutting out the opposition the first two games

"Hey, if we don't, it's gonna be one helluva year!"

On the 1979 San Diego play-off game

"You hear a lot about games being character builders. This was a character finder. Never in my thirty-one years of coaching have I seen one like it."

86

"I don't see how you can say one football team is intense and another isn't. Running around, patting everybody on the head, and jumping up and down doesn't mean they're intense."

On having his hat stolen in Pittsburgh for the second year in a row

"I have more respect for the guy last year who stole it off my head. It doesn't take much talent to grab one off a table."

On a Cliff Parsley fake punt:

"I'll have to let him know about our fine for running when you're supposed to punt. It's one thousand dollars—if you don't get the first down."

"This team is like a good pinch hitter. If he gets one strike, then another strike, then gets a single to the opposite field, nobody remembers the two strikes. We never seem to get that third strike."

Bum greets Mike Barber after defeating Dallas, 1979

On a feud with Dan Pastorini

"This thing was sort of like a lovers' quarrel. Once it was over, everything was better than before."

"We kissed and made up—not literally."

On players' missing practice

"If practice wasn't important, we wouldn't have it. We'd play on Sundays and take the rest of the week off."

On finding the air conditioning turned off in his office after a pre-season loss, 1975

"Hey, we didn't lose by *that* much."

Why his team doesn't scrimmage in training camp

"The Oilers aren't on the Oilers' schedule."

Bum with Dan Pastorini

"There are only two reasons for missing tackles. One, because you're scared. Two, because you're trying too hard. There's not anybody scared on this team."

On player salaries

"If you watch them play in the ice and snow in Cleveland in December, you don't think they're overpaid. If you see them get blind-sided and knocked into the third row, you don't think they're overpaid. Now, if you see them on the beach somewhere, in the summertime, then you might think they're overpaid."

On calling practice off during training camp due to lightning

"I've got some influence now, but not *that* much. What if it struck some of our *good* players, or the head coach?"

On Elvin Bethea and Curley Culp

"They're not the guys who usually get hurt. They're what you call hurters, not hurtees."

"Like my ol' high school coach told me. One day I asked, 'What do I hit 'em with, my left shoulder or my right?' My ol' coach said, 'I don't care if you hit 'em with your ass, long as you hit 'em hard.' "

On playing Cleveland

"They are like playing yourself. Same defense. Same gun. Same dog."

Vs. Los Angeles, 1978

"Four years ago, nobody would have bet we could stay on the field with Los Angeles. Now we lose by four points to a team five straight years in the play-offs, and everybody's mad as hell. I guess that's a compliment."

Asked whether he would be a spectator at the 1979 Super Bowl

"The only way to go to the Super Bowl is with a bench pass."

On the possibility of bad weather for an upcoming game

"There ain't but one guy who can do anything about it, and He ain't speaking to us. Not yet anyhow."

"There's an old saying that it's all right to cry a little bit, but not in public."

On going "by the book"

"Maybe I would, if I knew what the book is. I've never seen the book. I don't know who wrote it. Until I actually get my hands on it, I'll just have to go on using my own common sense."

"Flu doesn't keep you from playing football. It just makes you uncomfortable. If you're sick, you can always call time out, throw up, and keep on playing."

Oilers vs. Patriots, 1979

"The hardest thing in coaching? It's telling people they can't play no more. Or having to tell them you feel like you've got to trade 'em. You just can't get around that. You have to do what's best for everybody concerned. I hate it, but that doesn't mean I won't do it."

On rookie speedster Robert Woods

"It won't take long for him to get in good shape. At 165 pounds he doesn't have a lot of excess weight. In fact, he doesn't have a lot of excess anything."

"You can't evaluate a man who didn't have a chance. It's just like sending a man to a shooting match without a rifle."

Asked if he had any changes for the next game, after defeating Washington, score, 1979

"I want everything to stay the same, including the score."

On the NFL's practice of using part-time officials

"If I had my choice, I would like to see the league hire full-time officials. It would cost more money, but I think it's becoming necessary to make them responsible for their work. The way it is now, they can go back to their insurance business or whatever it is they do. I don't have an insurance business. If an official can cost me my job, I'd like to be able to cost him his."

"Coaching style doesn't have anything to do with dropping footballs or motion penalties. Whatever my coaching style is, if it will work when you win, it will work when you lose."

"Way back when I was coaching in high school I said I was going to play the one that deserved to play, no matter if he was white, black, brown, red, or what have you; that it wouldn't make any difference if he was the president of the school board's son or who he was. And I've managed to stick to that and believe it is the only way you do it. At least it's the only way I can do it and live with myself."

"The only guys who don't throw interceptions are the guys who don't throw, period."

RENFRO
82
SIDE JUDGE
14

On the infamous no-touchdown call, vs. Pittsburgh, January 1980

"If coaches have to live with what they do, then the officials should too. When I was a kid and came home after doing something wrong, I knew to go and cut a switch for my daddy. If they were raised like I was, there should have been a whole lot of switch-cutting Sunday."

On all the controversial calls going against the Oilers, 1977

"If there's a law of averages, then I should go undefeated the next two years."

On his own humor

"I've always said these things. Only when I was at Nederland High School, people weren't coming around and asking me questions."

"Your most successful teams are those whose average players play good and whose good players play great week after week. That's how you win. It's when your average players play mediocre and your good ones play average that you find yourself in trouble. Unfortunately, there's no way to know when that's going to happen."

No-touchdown call, Pittsburgh, 1980

Admitting that due to quarrels with officials, he calls the league office regularly

"I talk to Helen [his wife] too, and that does about as much good."

Asked why the Chicago Bears employed a certain coverage against the Oilers

"I don't know, I'm having hell answering the questions about *our* team."

On whether a questionable call in Cincinnati kept the Oilers out of the play-offs in 1977

"Have I ever thought about that? Oh, maybe four or five thousand times."

In his first season, 1975

"We've got to hold the rope."

We Love
the OILERS

On fan support

"A couple of times I wish they'd been on the field. You can't put it on the scoreboard. There's no point differential, but it's there. It's like looking for something in a guy's expense account. It's there if you can find it."

On the Oilers' 31–10 win over Cleveland, 1979

"We were too far ahead, even for us to catch up."

"We're building for the future, which is the right way. I want the Oilers to be good three years from now. I don't want anybody to inherit a team like I did."

"I've got a lot to be thankful about. There's nothing I'd rather be than a head football coach in the NFL, and there's definitely no place I'd rather be than in Houston. Down here's my home."

When asked why he doesn't wear his hat in the Astrodome

"I was always taught not to wear my hat indoors."

"Even old football coaches need love."

"I don't mind teams catching up on us, that is, as long as they don't catch up even."

"One of the lessons you learn in high school that you can't learn anywhere else is not to give up on kids. Kids that may not be much one year may be great the next year. Same in pro ball. They may not have done well for you one week, but they might do a heckuva job for you the next week if you don't give up on them."

On bad calls in San Francisco, 1978

"I was looking for my pocketknife. I was gonna cut my throat."

Oilers vs. Jets, 1979

1979
KEY HOUSTONIAN OF THE YEAR
O. A. "Bum" Phillips
PRESENTED BY THE
HOUSTON BOARD OF REALTORS

Helen Phillips on Bum

"I've often said I'd get more attention from him if I looked more like a football."

"We call him John Wayne—he kisses his horse."

After playing Pittsburgh, 1976

"Ever been to a circus when the bears got loose? The people scatter. That was us out there the second half."

After playing Pittsburgh, 1979

"We jumped offsides on the first play of the game. It got worse from there."

"Believe me, players can tell if you're counterfeit, no matter which way it is. Hell, just be yourself and the damn thing takes care of itself."

"You talk about experience, but some kinds of experience you don't need—like getting whipped."

Bum and Helen Phillips

"Folks have an image of what a coach ought to be, how he ought to look and talk. They expect to hear a lot of algebra from him. But football isn't that complicated. You push. The other team pushes back. The one that pushes hardest wins."

On his son, Wade, breaking his leg in high school where Bum was his coach

"It was the maddest my wife has been at me in all our years of marriage. What I did was buy Wade some barbells, and one night I brought them home and said, 'Here, as long as you're laid up in bed you might as well take these and build up your upper body.' Boy, did Helen get mad. But heck, he didn't have nothing to do laying there in bed."

On hiring Wade as defensive line coach

"Negotiate? There wasn't any negotiating to it. I just showed Wade the contract and said, 'This is it.' Just like I'd tell him what to eat for breakfast. After all, if he can't trust his ol' daddy, who can he trust?"

On the possibility of firing Wade

"After all, how can I fire him? If I fire him, I gotta fire my wife, my daughter-in-law, and my grandchildren."

"If a guy's got an acre, he's not going to fight as hard as a guy whose back's to the wall. When you're cornered you hit a whole lot harder."

"I've seen baseball pitchers walk in the winning run on four straight pitches, and that's with no rush. Sometimes the ball just doesn't go right where you want it to."

On the importance of intelligence in football

"If he can count to four, he can play for me."

On Don Shula

"Shula can take his'n and beat your'n, or he can take your'n and beat his'n."

"I like people and I don't mind them knowing it. Some coaches feel that if a player is too close to them he will take advantage of him. Personally I'd much rather have someone I like taking advantage of me than someone I don't like doing it."

On 1980 top draft choice Angelo Fields (6'6", 347 lbs.)

"He's not overweight, he's just overbig."

"I like standing next to Angelo. He makes me feel like I'm losing weight."

Asked if Angelo has his boots yet

"Where Angelo comes from they don't have enough cows to make boots that big."

Asked if Angelo could get down to about 260 lbs.

"His bones weigh that much."

Asked how his Oilers planned to counter Pittsburgh's awsome defense, 1975

"Besides prayer?"

On playing the Steelers

"Against that defense, a man ought to be able to carry a weapon."

"They just kicked us."

"I won't say it's a pleasure to play Pittsburgh. It's an honor. You know you're gonna have a heckuva fight on your hands. When that fight is over its kinda like when you had fights with your brother and sister. You work your business out and go back to likin' each other. That's kinda like the Oiler-Steeler rivalry has been."

"When we play them it's not a game—it's a collision. The team with the most band-aids wins."

"It's kinda like getting an ice cream cone on a hot day. You know, before you can get it all in your mouth it's all over you."

"We'd play the Steelers the same way if we're 1–13. We play them for the right to say we beat them, not for any championship."

On the Oilers' 24–17 victory over Pittsburgh on Monday Night Football, 1978

"We might have thrilled a nation, but we scared hell out of ourselves."

58
73

After turning down a man's offer of a specially heated bench for the Oilers' 1980 play-off in Pittsburgh

"But he didn't have a whip to go along with it to drive 'em out and play."

After losing to Pittsburgh in the play-offs, 1979

"The behinder we got, the worser it got."

After a loss to Pittsburgh, 1975

"I've got no complaints, except the score."

"I must be a good football coach because everybody here agrees with what I'm doing. Like shorter practices and fewer fines."

On the Oilers' toughness

"Pittsburgh has that reputation [of being tough]. After our game, I bet their lumps were bigger than ours."

Oilers vs. Pittsburgh, 1979

On Gregg Bingham

"To keep him out of a game you'd have to cut off his head and hide it."

To local writers

"When I die I want y'all to put a P.S. on my tombstone: 'He'd have lived a helluva lot longer if he hadn't had to play the Steelers six times in two years.'"

On the Oiler-Steeler AFC play-off game, 1980

"I don't see any snow. As far as I'm concerned it's seventy-two degrees and sunny, just like it is in Houston. We have no excuses, and we don't want any."

On trailing Pittsburgh 31–3 at halftime of the 1978 AFC play-off

"I don't think Billy Graham could have brought us back."

Gregg Bingham (54) wrestles Franco Harris (32)

To the press after the Oilers' win over Dallas, 1979

"Remember how I told you guys last week that this was just another game? I lied."

"If they're America's team, we must be Texas' team."

On the Dallas Cowboys

"The team up north of here, I can't think of their name."

"You don't go looking for excuses for your problems; you look for solutions. Hell, what's happened has happened. When a guy hits you in the mouth, you don't stop to find out why; you hit him back and then ask the questions."

Vs. Dallas, 1976

"We got too cautious in the end. We didn't let them have the bomb, but, well, two hand grenades add up to one bomb."

On Ted Washington

"He's wide and slung low. He's just like one of those old cement irrigation tanks. You're not gonna get the ground he's on. He's some stout."

"Moving Teddy is like trying to push over the First National Bank."

On Dan Pastorini

"If this kid didn't have bad luck, he wouldn't have any luck at all."

On Jimmy Young as a rookie

"He don't always know where the ball's going, but he's sure as hell interested in finding out."

"An all-Texas Super Bowl? The world isn't ready for that. If you think we're obnoxious now. . ."

Greg Bingham (54) and Ted Washington (59)

On Carl Mauk

"Anybody who doesn't think football is life and death better check with Carl. You step on that field and you're invading his territory."

After Carl Mauk broke his rib during summer camp

"Carl, you have thirteen ribs; what difference does one make?"

On the Leon Gray acquisition

"We were looking for the best possible trade without getting robbed. The way it turned out, we did the robbing."

"The first time he came off the ball, he popped the tackle, ricocheted off and boom, cut the linebacker, just like he did for New England. What's he gonna be like when he gets his timing down?"

"I'd say he's capable of learning our system completely in a short while. In most cases it's block the feller closest to you."

Carl Mauk

On Toni Fritsch

"I'll tell you one thing, every time I see that kid going onto the field, I thank God for our country's immigration laws."

On Toni Fritsch's loose-fitting pants

"Looks like a Dutch family moved out of the back of those britches."

On Toni Fritsch's game-winning field goal vs. Cincinnati, 1979

"Those Cincinnati fans were hollerin', but that didn't bother him. As well as he understands English, he might have thought they were cheering him."

"I'd rather have a good high school coaching job than a lousy pro coaching job."

Toni Fritsch

On Earl Campbell

"I wouldn't say Earl is in a class by himself, but I'll tell you one damn thing: It don't take them long to call the roll."

"Earl Campbell ain't like those high-priced, spoiled athletes. Why, he had me over to his office the other day, just like one of the guys. And he said he didn't believe it was my fault we didn't win in the play-offs either."

"I've never known anyone in all my years of being around football more deserving of all these titles, records, and awards he's won."

His report on Earl Campbell after an injury

"Earl's walking better, but he's much more valuable to this team if he can run."

On Earl's 81-yard touchdown run vs. Miami, 1978

"That ruined our plan. We just wanted a first down so we could run the clock out."

"Fortunately, only eleven at a time could tackle him, but it seemed like all eleven were on him all night."

Bum with injured Earl Campbell

When asked about Earl Campbell's taking a long time to get back up after being tackled

"Earl's slow getting up, but he's also slow going down."

On Billy Johnson

"Billy Johnson is by far the best return man I've ever seen and the best one I ever want to see, because if I see anybody else he's gonna be on somebody's else's team."

"Billy's an equal opportunity runner. He gives everybody an equal chance to tackle him."

On Billy Johnson's wearing two pairs of panty hose to keep warm.

"No, I didn't wear them Sunday or any other day. I think I would just go ahead and get cold. But, if Billy wants to wear them, I'll help him put them on."

On Johnson's 1978 contract hold-out

"It would probably cost me my job. I don't want to be like the kid who found out there wasn't a Santa Claus. I believe in Santa Claus and Billy Johnson."

Billy Johnson

“We’ve got to learn to hammer the teams we’re supposed to. We’ve got to put the kill shot on them, really dump them. That’s the one thing I want to change about this football team. I want to see us play as good against the weaker teams as we do against the good ones.”

“It’s a lot easier to coach in the play-offs; it’s just tougher to get there.”

At the Oiler appreciation rally January 6, 1980

“I’d like to tell you why I don’t want to talk—because I’m cryin’.

“I said there’s no way they can top the reception we had last year, but let me tell you one damn thing, you’ve topped it.

“This year I said the road to the Super Bowl went through Pittsburgh. I’ll tell you one damn thing—next year the road to the Super Bowl goes through Houston.

“One year ago we knocked on the door.

“This year we beat on the door.

“Next year we’re gonna kick the son-of-a-bitch in!”

Sources:
Austin American-Statesman
Dallas Morning News
Houston Chronicle
Houston Post
Los Angeles Times
New York Times
Pittsburgh Press
Sports Illustrated
Associated Press
United Press International
KPRC/Channel 2, Houston